INDIANS AND THE U.S. CONSTITUTION:

A FORGOTTEN LEGACY

by

Kirke Kickingbird

Lynn Shelby Kickingbird

CONTENTS

INTRODUCTION
1

FOUNDATION OF DEMOCRACY
2

WAR AND PEACE
10

SHAPING THE CONSTITUTION
18

INDIANS UNDER THE CONSTITUTION
26

BIBLIOGRAPHY
34

ABOUT THE AUTHORS
35

PRODUCTION

RESEARCH ASSOCIATE: *Beth Berlin-Greb*
*Institute for the Development
of Indian Law*

DESIGN: *Ben Crenshaw*
Lithographics, Washington, D.C.

TYPESETTING: *Ray Weiss*
Lithographics, Washington, D.C.

PRINTING: *Welsh Printing Corp.,
Falls Church, VA*

Sponsors

Administration for Native Americans,
U.S. Department of Health and Human Services

Baltimore American Indian Center

The Native American Committee of
the Presbyterian Church in the USA

Dr. Cecil Corbett, Director, Cook Christian
Theological School, Tempe, Arizona

LaDonna Harris, President, Americans for
Indian Opportunity, Washington, D.C.

Cover features Medicine Crow, Crow Tribe, 1880

PAGE 3 "Council of State," Engraving by Theodor de Bry, after original by Jacques le Moyne de Morgues in Nicolas Le Challeux's narrative of Capt. Jean Ribaut's last voyage to Florida, c. 1565, Smithsonian Institution. **4** Hiawatha Wampum Belt, New York State Museum. **7** "The Town of Secaton," engraving by Theordo de Bry after original painting by John White, appearing in 1590 edition of Thomas Hariot's report "...on Virginia," Smithsonian Institution. **9** U.S. Treaty with Shawnee & others, 1786, National Archives. **11** "A Draught of the Creek Nation," William Bonar, 1757, British Museum, London. **13** "Kicking Bird," by Soule, 1870, Div. of Manuscripts, Univ. of Okla. Library. **17** Osceola, Seminole, Smithsonian Institution. **19** Cherokee Chiefs in London, 1762, engraving, Colonial Williamsburg. **21** Chief Tomochichi and Nephew, Smithsonian Institution. **22** Camp of Piekanns, National Archives, U.S. Signal Corps. **23** Creek leader in New York, sketches by John Trumbull, Smithsonian Institution. **25** Austenaco, Cherokee engraving, Smithsonian Institution. **27** Indian delegation to Washington, 1857, by Mathew Brady, U.S. Signal Corps, National Archives. **29** "Grand Rush advertisement, Kansas City, 1879, Library of Congress. **32** Painting of Tahlequah Council, 1843, by John Mix Stanley, Smithsonian Institution. **33** Black Hills Expedition, W.H. Illingworth, 1874, National Archives. **34** Chief Plenty Coups, National Archives, U.S. Signal Corps.

INTERNATIONAL STANDARD BOOK NUMBER 0-944253-87-3
COPYRIGHT© 1987 Kirke Kickingbird & Lynn Shelby Kickingbird
PUBLISHED by Institute for the Development of Indian Law, Inc., Washington, D.C.

INTRODUCTION

Washington, D.C. is at its most popular during the summer months. But every visitor to the nation's capital, no matter what the season, has on his list of sights to see, the Nation's Capitol. The Dome of the Capitol is the symbol that signifies Washington and Congress and the government of the United States. On the very top of the Capitol Dome stands a twenty foot tall figure. The majestic bronze statue is clothed in robes and wears an eagle headress. None of its features can be seen clearly three hundred feet below in front of the east side of the Capitol. But it is always a cause of wonder and both residents and tourists can be heard to ask, "Who is that Indian?"

The figure brings to mind every chief astride his horse on the hill on the horizon. It brings to mind every warrior silhouetted against the bluff. Who is that magnificent and powerful Indian on top of the Capitol? It is not an Indian. But it probably should have been. It is the purpose of this book to tell you why! The figure on top of the Capitol is Freedom.

Why should magnificence and power and freedom be mistaken for an Indian? Because these qualities are only part of what the Indian people gave to the people who came to America. This book is going to tell you about the impact Indian people had on the newcomers and on the United States Constitution, and the impact the Constitution has had on the Indian nations. It begins long ago at a time in which only the Indians were called Americans.

Nor have I been able to learn whether they held personal property, for it seemed to me that whatever one had, they all took shares of.... They are so ingenuous and free with all they have, that no one would believe it who has not seen it; of anything that they possess, if it be asked of them, they never say no; on the contrary they invite you to share it and show as much love as if their hearts went with it....
—Christopher Columbus,
after returning from his first voyage

THE INDIAN FOUNDATIONS OF DEMOCRACY

When the Spanish, French and English explored the East Coast of the United States in the early 1500s there were over one hundred tribes and bands of Indians living between the Atlantic Ocean and the Mississippi River. Each one of these directly or indirectly affected the foundations of the United States Government. America remembers that the "discovery" of the New World revealed great wealth, new commodities and new trade routes, but America forgets that the greatest revelation of the European "discovery" was a new concept of social organization and government which would change the course of history.

On certain days each year the Timicuan Indians of 16th century Florida met in a "council of state" to discuss important affairs.

WE THE PEOPLE

The idea that governmental authority springs from the will of the people was not invented by the Englishman, Locke, or the Frenchman, Rousseau. John Locke's *First and Second Treatise on Government* had appeared in 1690 setting forth the idea that the people of a nation contract with a ruler or king to govern them. Jean-Jacques Rousseau's *Social Contract* (1762) viewed the basis for government as an agreement by the people not with a king, but with themselves to combine their individual will into the General Will.

The yeast for this intellectual ferment was the encounter with the American Indian. Ideas about the "ideal government" were not derived from an active imagination, but from actual events. American Indians were seen as the embodiment of the spirit of freedom. The writings of Amerigo Vespucci *(Mundus Novus* or *New World,* 1505), and interviews with the Dutch explorers who had visited America and the Indians gave St. Thomas More his vision for the book *Utopia* (1516) with its government operating on the consent of the governed.

The Spanish explorer, Peter Martyr, wrote his American history, *Decades of the New World,* in Latin in 1516. It was translated into English in 1555. European intellectuals viewed Martyr's Golden World of the Indian as the ideal state of which the ancient Greek and Roman writers and philosophers spoke. The description intrigued the mind of Montaigne. Montaigne read the books and writings of the European explorers, interviewed as many as he could, and talked with three Indians touring Europe at the Court of King Charles IX in 1562. The Indians commented on the injustice of European society with its classes of rich and poor. Drawing on these interviews and using part of Martyr's history,

Montaigne wrote his essay on the New World, entitled "Of the Cannibals" (1578–80) in which he discussed the ideal country and its government.

The intellectual environment in which men like Voltaire, More, Montaigne, Shakespeare, Hobbes, Locke, Bentham and Rousseau lived and breathed was saturated with the influence of New World government, but only a few knew its American Indian foundations and fewer still would inquire.

The intellectual thought of Locke's time, however, confined the "People" to the wealthy class. It would take a continuing direct encounter with the New World before that concept would broaden to include all citizens in a democratic society.

For the moment, we are concerned about the American Indian people who viewed government as a servant of the people rather than the people as a servant of the king. They had been operating their governments for centuries on principles that European writers would describe when they put pen to paper. Over and over the journals and correspondence of early explorer's confirm the Indians' passion for "government by the people." But who were the people in the minds of the Indians?

The majority of Indian nations throughout what is now the United States defined "The People" through their own name for themselves, "The People," "The Real People," the "The Principle People." The concept behind this positive self-image defined social, cultural, political, and economic relationships. Through these relationships, the community would uphold the rights of the individual, but the individual could not place his own needs above those of the community. This balance between individual liberty and the general welfare was effectively maintained by tribal belief systems which incorporated rigid codes of personal morality with a keen sense of community responsibility.

LEADERSHIP

Indian political leadership was as different from contemporary European forms as night and day. The Indian leader was both a "ruler" and a "servant" whose primary role was to preserve harmony and secure the welfare of the nation. Another distinctly "American" trait, is seen in the fact that North American tribes did not sanction the concept of absolute rule. Among the Iroquois, for example, there was no single, monarchial ruler, but a group of representative leaders closely tied to the People through its kinship, clan and legal systems. Tribes, like the Cherokee and Choctaw, had principal or paramount chiefs who ruled *with the advice and consent of a council*. The principal chief was at once responsible for the welfare of all the parts of a confederation and subject to the individual leaders of each town, band or community.

In an effort to maintain a balance and minimize the possibility for self-aggrandizement, most tribal civil and military leaders distributed their wealth among the members and thus, were generally poorer than the citizenry. According to the 18th century historian, Cadwallader Colden, "If they [Indian leaders] should be once suspected of selfishness they would grow mean in the opinion of their Country-men, and would consequently lose their authority."

The Great Binding Law of the Iroquois referenced the qualities required for leadership:

The lords of the Confederacy of Five Nations shall be mentors of the people for all time. The thickness of their skins shall be seven spans, which is to say that they shall be proof against anger, offensive action and criticism. Their hearts shall be full of peace and good will and their minds filled with a yearning for the welfare of the people of the confederacy. With endless patience they shall carry out their duties and their firmness shall be tempered with a tenderness for their people. Neither anger nor fury shall find lodgement in their minds and all their words and actions shall be marked by calm deliberation.

Hiawatha Wampum Belt signifying the forming of the League of the Five Nations Iroquois Confederacy. Hundreds of Iroquois wampum belts represented treaties and laws.

ELECTIONS

The manner by which chiefs were selected or elected differed from tribe to tribe. The U.S. Constitution provided that electors select the President and state legislators select the senators. The Iroquois system was partially hereditary, partially electoral with provision for the selection of "pine-tree chiefs" by virtue of their ability. Ethnologist Louis Henry Morgan, in his *League of the Iroquois* (1851) says:

It seems to have been the aim of the Ho-de-no-sau-nee

to avoid the dangers of an hereditary transmission of power, without fully adopting the opposite principle of a free election founded upon merit and capacity. . . . Their system was a modification of the two opposite rules. . . .

The Iroquois constitution also included a definite role for women in the election process by providing for the nomination of leaders to the Great Council by the Clan mothers from all five tribes.

One of the most economically successful tribes of the 17th and 18th centuries was the Choctaw who occupied millions of acres along the Gulf Coast and produced bushels of surplus crops each year. Divided into three governmental districts representing distinct geographic areas, the Choctaw's democratic government provided for a *mingo,* a principle chief who was elected by the men of each district. Factors that aided the election of *mingos* were characteristics we recognize in the modern American politician: family history, administrative skill, and military achievement.

Whatever the process for selection or election, common to most native governments was the principle that leaders who did not maintain the confidence of the community or in any way violated its trust, were quickly deposed. The United States Constitution would recognize this as "impeachment."

LOCAL SELF-GOVERNMENT

Closely allied with government derived from the will of the people is the concept of local self-government. Although many Indian nations could be characterized as "federations" (a number of smaller units bound together into a central government by mutual consent), the primary focus of government among natives of the 16th to 18th centuries was their local town or band. These were the governments that affected the conduct of daily life, including the growing, foraging, hunting and storing of food, the education of the young, the maintenance of peace and harmony. These same endeavors occupied the colonial settlers. Only periodically would they come together at a central location for a grand council to celebrate and worship, to share information, to air grievances, and to discuss concerns about intratribal and international relations. Their state or nation resulted from a confederation of local governments who spoke a common language, shared a common history and tradition, and occupied a common territory for hunting and agriculture. The New England town meeting, the Continental Congress and the Articles of Confederation were the colonial counterparts of the centuries old Indian practice.

As practitioners of effective local self-government, the Indians became an example for men like Jefferson and Franklin. For others, like Alexander Hamilton, a concern for wisdom and schooling as the basis for governmental decision making and law making was preferable. The authoritarian, monarchial systems also were more consistent with European elitist tradition, and intended to protect the nation as a whole from the "tyranny of the masses" as de Toqueville termed it. In the end, the distinctly American brand of democracy would favor local self-government over strong, central, "expert" government.

LIBERTY AND EQUALITY

Regard for individual liberty was common among the Indians that the colonists encountered. It could be seen in their child rearing practices and in their governments where each person had a voice. To the Indian the idea of imprisonment or confinement as a penalty for a crime was unknown. To the Indian, death was preferable to imprisonment.

Integral to the concept of personal liberty is the notion of equality. Indians coulb not be subjugated as slaves, as some of the early tobacco farmers had tried to the Indians' horror. Indeed, those few that were enslaved would often escape, taking with them any negroes who would come. Even after battle, the victorious tribe would agree to nationalize their captives as long as the latter promised to abide by the laws of the nation.

Many writers of colonial times noted the Indians' love for freedom. The Indians of the southeast were personified by historian, James Adair in his *History of the American Indians* published in 1775, as breathing "nothing but liberty."

Their love for freedom was contagious and by 1776 it was shared by a good many of the colonists as noted in this *History of North & South America* published in England that year.

The darling passion of the American is liberty and that in its fullest extent; nor is it the original natives only to whome this passion is confined; our colonists sent thither seem to have imbibed the same principles.

GOVERNMENT

It is common among historians to describe Indian nations as having inadequate governments or no government. Upon reading colonial journals and ethnohistories, however, one is amazed at how such conclusions could be reached. Writers from 1492 on provide detailed descriptions of

Indian government. Such a bias is obviously due to a divergent view of what the purpose of life and government is, as Benjamin Franklin explained:

Savages we call them because their manners differ from ours which we think the perfection of civility; they think the same of theirs.... Our laborious manner of life, compared with theirs, they esteem slavish and base; and the learning on which we value ourselves they regard as frivolous and useless.

According to historian Francis Jennings, "it was not the absence of Indian government that baffled the British, but rather the effective resistance to subjection by the stubbornly existing governments."

What is clear is that Indian governments were very different from those in Europe. The style of leadership and the role the people played was contradictory to the European tradition. The primary focus of relatively small, local self-governments coming together into a grand council periodically as needs or custom required contrasted with the oppressive, authoritarian style of European monarchies. And, unlike the European societies, the operational and philosophical rules pertaining to American Indian government promoted individual liberty and equality for the sake of the common good.

In *Remarks Concerning the Savages of North America*, Benjamin Franklin described Native American constitutions as follows:

The Indian men, when young, are hunters and warriors; when old, counsellors; for all their government is by counsel of the sages; there is no force, there are no prisons, no officers to compel obedience or inflict punishment. Hence they generally study oratory, the best speaker having the most influence. The Indian women till the ground, dress the food, nurse and bring up the children, and preserve and hand down to posterity the memory of public transactions. These employments of men and women are accounted natural and honourable. Having few artificial wants, they have abundance of leisure for improvement by conversation.

CONSTITUTIONS

Until the ratification of the United States Constitution no nation-state operated under a written constitution. The British Constitution is not a single written document like the United States Constitution. It consists of the Magna Carta, statutes of Parliament, judicial decisions and principles of common law. The American Indian tribes had unwritten, traditional law or "common law" like the Anglo-Saxon tribes. It was because American Indian "common law" was unwritten that many historians and policy makers refused to acknowledge the existence of constitutions, laws and governments among Indian nations.

The historical and anthropological evidence strikingly points to well established rules of custom and tradition practiced by native governments. The Five Nations of the Iroquois are the most prominent example with their Great Law of Peace which they carefully transmitted to tribal members and future generations through oral history and wampum belts. The design of these wampum belts were symbolic representations of constitutional principles and laws.

But other great Indian nations the Europeans first encountered also had unwritten constitutions, including many of the tribes of southern New England, the Delaware, the Cherokee, The Creek and The Choctaw.

THE CHEROKEE

The 18th century Cherokee were a hallmark of local self-government. While the nation met in central council to consider matters of war and alliance, it was the local town councils guided by well-established custom law which governed and ensured the general welfare. The achievement of harmony was the overriding goal. Men and women were free to air their grievances openly at town council meetings. Those sitting on the council worked to build a consensus after prolonged discussion, sometimes lasting several days.

THE CHOCTAW

The great agrarian nation of the Choctaw, whose territory extended over thirteen million acres encompassing parts of Alabama and Louisiana and almost all of Mississippi, had an interesting and unusual political system. Each of the three geographic sections of the tribe had their own *mingo,* or principal

---

Such was the spirit of the Iroquois system of government, that the influence of the inferior chiefs, the warriors, and even of the women would make itself felt, whenever the subject itself aroused a general public interest.
—Lewis Henry Morgan, Ethnologist, from *League of the Iroquois,* 1851.

This de Bry engraving appearing in a 1590 report on Virginia by Thomas Hariot shows the elaborate town of "Secota," near present-day Bremerton, North Carolina, with its cornfields, groves of trees, and general village life.

7

chief. Much like a modern-day state governor, the elected *mingo* was responsible for the government within his region. Helping him to carry out the laws and policies were captains and sub-chiefs, mayor-like leaders of the towns and villages.

From time to time, a national council meeting would be called on a day agreed upon by the three mingos. The three districts would alternate hosting the meeting which was held in the village square of the host. Elaborate pre-council ceremonies included passing the pipe and extensive prayer. The council meeting began with a speech usually given by the host chief's *tichou mingo* (servant of the chief) who served his chief much like an executive assistant. He would explain to the delegates the reason for calling the meeting and the issues as he and his chief saw them.

Any delegate could voice his opinion on a subject without any limitation to time. After all views were aired on a subject, the host mingo carefully considered them in a concluding statement. At the end of each sentence he waited for the voice approval of the delegates.

THE IROQUOIS

No other form of Indian government has been studied as much as the League of the Iroquois and its Great Law of Peace whose existence can be traced back over 500 years and whose origins are obscured with age. The Five Nations of the Iroquois League had their own internal tribal governments led by chiefs elected by hereditary clans. It was not until they formed the Confederacy, however, that the nations individually and collectively reached their political and military peak. Under the League, or the *Ho-de-no-sau-ne,* the Five Nations ruled their affairs through a polity (rule by a large body of select citizens) under a comprehensive system of fixed, democratic laws. The laws were committed to memory and represented by a specific wampum belt or string of beads. The keepers of the wampum were expected to study and know the law and be well-versed in its interpretation.

Like the other tribal governments mentioned, the Iroquois' Great Council or *Ho-de-os'-seh* only met when the need arose. Such occasions might include the selection of a new chief, the declaration of war, and the forming of political and economic alliances. If the reason was compelling enough, old, young, women, and men left their hunting grounds from as far away as Tennessee or Virginia to witness the council. For the official leaders, attendance was compulsory.

The nature of these council meetings is vividly portrayed by Lewis Henry Morgan in his *League of the Iroquois:*

Among the Indian nations whose ancient seats were within the limits of our republic, the Iroquois have long continued to occupy the most conspicuous position. They achieved for themselves a more remarkable civil organization and acquired a higher degree of influence than any race of Indian lineage, except those of Mexico and Peru.

But more important than the ceremonies and the oratory associated with them, or, for that matter, their operating procedures, are the nature of the laws which comprised the Iroquois constitution. In the brief list below, it is easy to see how the Great Law of the Iroquois must have influenced the Founding Fathers.

American Democratic Foundations In the Great Law of Peace

Democratic unicameral parliamentary-type government
Freedom of religion
Separation of politics and religion
Separation of civil and military governments
Concept of checks and balances
Veto
Referendum
Amendment to the Great Law
Protection against unlawful entry

In 1727, Cadwallader Colden published the first book on the League's social and political system, *History of the Five Indian Nationa Depending on the Province of New York in America.* In it he said:

Each nation is an absolute Republick by itself, govern'd in all Publick affairs of War and Peace by the Sachems of Old Men, whose Authority and Power

---

It will be said, that great societies cannot exist without government. The savages, therefore, break them into small ones.
—Thomas Jefferson, *Notes on Virginia,* 1801.

is gained by and consists wholly in the opinions of the rest of the Nation in their Wisdom and Integrity. They never execute their Resolutions by Compulsion or Force Upon any of their People. Honour and Esteem are their pincipal Rewards, as Shame and being Despised are their punishments.

The Iroquois confederacy was so effective at maintaining harmony among the Six Nations that they remained the most powerful national force east of the Mississippi throughout the 16th, 17th and most of the 18th century. When colonial representatives met with the Six Nations at Lancaster, Pennsylvania in 1744, the Iroquois Chief, Canasatego, gave this sage advice to the colonies on forming a united government:

Our Wise forefathers established Union and Amity between the Five Nation. This has... given us great Weight and Authority with our neighboring Nations.... And by your observing the same Methods our Wise Forefathers have taken, you will acquire such Strength and Power.

CONCLUSION

With colonization, the newcomers to American shores would begin a process that would lead to a new definition of "The People" in North America. The "Americans," a term that was then applied only to the Indians, would be caught up in that process of definition.

The process would be guided by European intellectuals who had been dazzled by the revelation of a new kind of government in America. It was not the king but the people who were the focus of the "new" American government. The American government represented liberty, equality, and the consent of the governed. The American ideas set to paper by European writers would change the expectations of generations and the course of history. It was all built on the Indian foundations of democracy.

U.S. Treaty of peace and cession with the Shawnee, Wyandat and Delaware, January, 1786. It clarified the states of Indian lands formerly claimed by England and France.

...And when there is equality of condition, manners and privileges, and a constant familiarity in society, as prevails in every Indian nation, and through all our British colonies, there glows such a cheerfulness and warmth of courage in each of their breasts, as cannot be described.

—James Adair, Historian, 1775.

"During the course of a long life in which I have made observations of public affairs, it has appeared to me that almost every war between the Indians and whites has been occasioned by some injustice of the latter towards the former."
—Benjamin Franklin on the causes of Indian wars.

WAR AND PEACE

The influence of the American Indian was everywhere in colonial America. The Indian was a factor in the political, economic, military, and territorial aspects of the lives of the colonists. From the food on the table to the bars on the door, to the allies and enemies beyond the walls of the stockade, every waking or sleeping man, woman or child knew that every facet of their lives was shaped by Indians.

The pervasive Indian presence required the development of an Indian policy first by Spain, eventually by Britain and her colonies, and finally by the United States. The various policies would affect trading relations, land acquisition, political and military alliances, and legal institutions. The issues were so interwoven that it is difficult to discuss them separately. The impressive military strength of the Indians had to be taken into consideration at every decision point. The colonists of Jamestown,

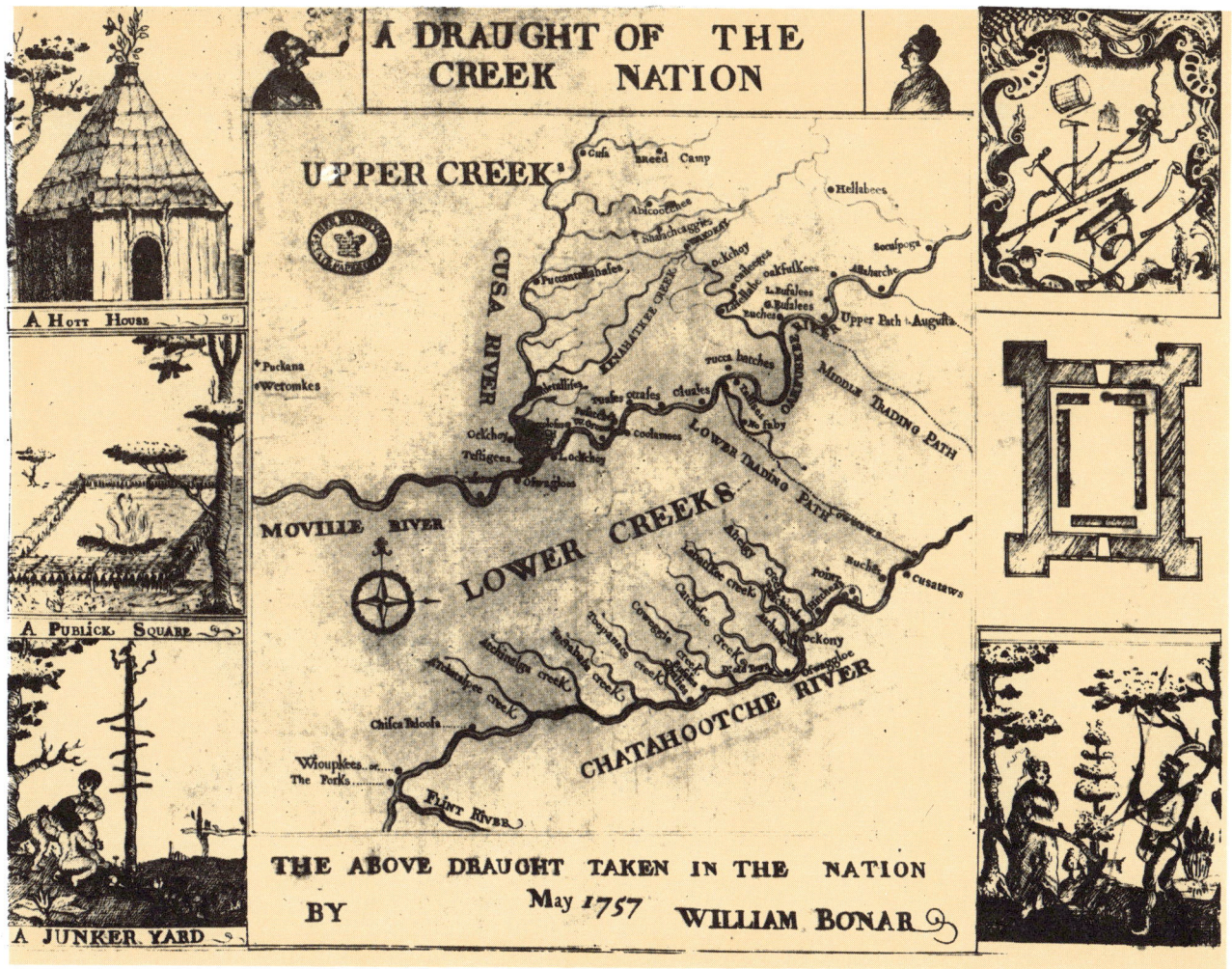

A 1757 manuscript map with border drawings of the Creek Nation by William Bonar, an aide to South Carolina Indian agent, Samuel Pepper. Both the British and French were vying for an alliance with the Creek at the time.

Quebec and Plymouth owed their existence to an appreciation and practice of diplomacy, but Sir Walter Raleigh's colony at Roanoke, repeatedly antagonized the Indians and disappeared.

AGGRESSORS OR DEFENDERS

Perhaps the most popular view of Indians is that of the "savage warrior." Indians were indeed skilled soldiers, employing tactics especially suitable to the dense forests of North American continent. Traditionally, native warfare was generally limited to the protection of towns and villages as well as food supplies and hunting grounds. As European trade became a common dynamic to tribal living, the protection of trade routes and commodities were causes for war.

The first major English colonial Indian war took place in Virginia and lasted for more than twenty years. Since the establishment of Jamestown as a British colony in 1607 the English and the Indians maintained a cordial relationship under Powhatan.

The English colonists ultimately created difficult pressures through their pilferage of Indian corn or their desperate insistence that the Indians should sell their corn. The peace became uneasy and the situation became explosive when, with the rise of tobacco as an export crop, the colonists increased demands for land to grow tobacco. With Powhattan's death in 1618, a strained relationship deteriorated into war when the

Powhatan Confederacy attacked Jamestown in 1622. When the fighting ended in 1644, the Powhatan Confederacy had been destroyed as a military and political force.

After Jamestown, English activity increased. In the 1620s two colonies were established at Plymouth and Salem in what was to become Massachusetts. English efforts to establish the Province of Maryland and the Colony of Connecticut were successful during the next decade. In 1663 a Carolina charter was granted by the British Crown claiming jurisdiction over territory from Daytona Beach, Florida to the southern border of Virginia. In 1664, the English took over the Dutch holdings in New Amsterdam as well as the Dutch fur trade with the Indians.

The Pequot leader, Metacom, urged the Indians of the New England area to rid their homelands of the invaders and led King Philip's War (1675-81). The Indians would be the loser's not only because of the ravages of disease, but also because of the alliance struck by the British with the Iroquois Confederacy.

THE LEAGUE OF THE IROQUOIS

The League of the Five Nations of the Iroquois Confederacy was founded some time between 1390 and 1500. Made up of the Mohawk, Onondaga, Seneca, Oneida, and Cayuga nations, five related but warring tribes. Under the leadership of Hiawatha, the Iroquois successfully struck a truce and formed a sophisticated government structure under a constitution known as the Great Law of Peace. Under the Great Law, the Iroquois thrived and expanded. In 1712 the Tuscarora of North Carolina joined the League, which then became known as the Six Nations.

Although physically based in the New York area, (the central fire or capitol of their government was at present-day Syracuse), the influence of the formidable Iroquois spread in all directions reaching west to the Mississippi River and south through Tennessee and Virginia. Its power to control the fur trade, land sales, a host of subordinate tribes, and peace or war compelled the attentions of both other tribes and the Europeans. The Dutch and the British appreciated the military and political strength of the Iroquois. The British prospered because of their alliance with the League.

The French failed to grasp the significance of the Five Nations soon enough. In 1609, Samuel Champlain attacked a group of Iroquois at Ticonderoga on Lake Champlain, and established an enmity that would set the stage for the British-Iroquois alliance that would dominate French, British and colonial ambitions in North America for the next two centuries.

In 1664, when Governor Stuyvesant surrendered New Netherlands to the British following a naval blockade of New Amsterdam, the British became allies of the Iroquois with the annexation of the Dutch Fort Orange. The Dutch position was probably hopeless before the English blockade. Dutch diplomacy with the Indians was so bad they had to build a wall at New Amsterdam on Manhattan Island to keep out "wolves and Indians." The only wolves feared today at this "Wall Street" are of the financial variety.

The British-Iroquois alliance effectively thwarted French territorial and fur trading ambitions. As the French prepared to expand their trade into New York and New England, the Iroquois renewed their allegiance to the English Crown on January 22, 1690. King Williams War, which began in February, 1690, resulted in the burning of Schenectady, New York and the raiding of numerous towns in Maine, New Hampshire and Massachusetts. In 1694, colonial representatives from Connecticut, Massachusetts, New Jersey, and New York signed a peace treaty with the Iroquois in Albany in order to prevent any future alliance between the Iroquois and the French. In 1722, Virginia Governor Alexander Spotswood negotiated a treaty of peace with the Iroquois. The Iroquois League was clearly an indispensable ally of the English colonies.

By the end of the 17th century, the English had succeeded in establishing strong, viable settlements and colonies up and down the Atlantic Coast—many on the sites of former Indian towns.

THE FRENCE AND ENGLISH FIGHT FOR DOMINION

In Europe during the latter part of the 17th century and the beginning of the 18th century, the French, British, Dutch, Spanish and Portuguese were embroiled in the War of the Spanish Succession which spread to the New World where it became known as Queen Anne's War (1701-1713). In North America the English fought the Spanish and the French over territorial boundaries in the Southeast. The wars ended with the Treaty of Utrecht in 1713 leaving the boundaries essentially the same. With Britain's renewed interest in her southern boundaries, the royal colony of Georgia was founded in 1733.

In the 1730s, the Indians allied with England in wars against Spain, again over the southern boundary. Like Queen Anne's War,

---

Nothing ought to be more avoided than the embarking ourselves in a system of military coercion on the Indians. If we do this, we shall have general and perpetual war.

—Thomas Jefferson in a letter to Meriwether Lewis, 1808

Kiowa chief Kicking Bird, signer of the Treaty of Medicine Lodge, 1867, was praised for his skills as warrior and diplomat.

the results left the southern boundary of the English territory the same but firmly established the French in the Louisiana Territory. The French had thus succeeded in their efforts to encircle the British colonies with the claims to Louisiana, the Northwest Territories, and Canada.

The British and the French emerged in the middle of the 18th century as the major contenders for the eastern territories. They had the advantage of thriving, diversified colonial economies and substantial populations. They had the disadvantage that their own colonists were beginning to become surly reformers kindling the fires of revolution. During the 18th century, pictorial representations of America in documents ranging from maps to political cartoons depict America as an Indian. The Indian ideas of freedom, liberty and government that had been circulated by philosophers like Locke and Rousseau were beginning to have effect and would ultimately take their toll on monarchy.

In 1753, the French Governor Duquesne closed the Ohio Country to the English by building a line of forts on the Allegheny and upper Ohio rivers. The governor of Virginia sent a protest, and then twenty-two-year-old Lieutenant Colonel George Washington and his Virginia Militia to chastise the French. The defeat of the Virginia Militia at Great Meadows near Ft. Duquesne in 1754 precipitated a crisis in Indian affairs. Could the British hold their Iroquois and other Indian allies?

With the start of the French and Indian War (1754-1763), the Iroquois were trying to judge whether a British or French alliance would have a higher value. The British Board of Trade instructed the royal colonial governors to meet the Six Nations at Albany and "secure their wavering friendship." The Iroquois chose to remain neutral, while other tribes sided with the French.

In 1755, General Braddock, commander in chief of the English forces in the American colonies, appointed Sir William Johnson Indian Commissioner. General Johnson, married to a Mohawk, was able to enlist the aid of the Iroquois in several decisive battles against the French, including the capture of the fort at Niagara. Convinced that land frauds in Indian country were the main cause of tribal unrest, Johnson advocated approval by the Indian commissioner of all Indian-white land transfers. In 1756, he was appointed Northern Commissioner of Indian Affairs.

With the end of the French and Indian War concluded by the signing of the Treaty of Paris (February, 1763), the English claimed sovereignty over the territory of the Indian allies of the French. Colonial encroachments on Indian lands began in the old Northwest Territory bounded by the Great Lakes, the Ohio, and the Mississippi rivers. Motivated by the land trespasses and unfavorable trade terms, the Ottawa chief, Pontiac, led the Indian allies of the French in a war to protect Indian interests. From May through July, 1763, Pontiac destroyed all the British garrisons west of Niagara (Forts Sandusky, Saint Joseph, Miami, Quiatenon, Venango, Le Beouf, and Duquesne), and beseiged Detroit and Fort Pitt. Although Pontiac was finally defeated, the level of unrest among the Indians required a major response from the British Government.

A NEW BRITISH INDIAN POLICY UNFOLDS

The new British Indian policy was set forth in October in the *Royal Proclamation of 1763* in which Great Britain recognized Indian rights, forbade settlement west of the Appalachians, reserved the land not ceded or purchased for the Indian nations or tribes, and required royal permission for any future purchase of Indian land. The purchase of any lands that the Indians wished to sell would take place at a public assembly.

To reduce the friction created by English colonial trespass on Indian lands, the terms of the Proclamation created a boundary line making the border of Indian country run from the eastern end of Lake Ontario to the Gulf of Mexico in northwest Florida. The boundary line was intended to be a barrier against western settlement by British subjects.

The Proclamation was not effective, and it was not popular with His Majesty's colonial subjects. It failed in its stated objectives due to the lack of enforcement. The problem that had long been apparent in British and colonial Indian affairs continued to plague the implementation of the new policy—there was no centralized control over Indian affairs in the colonies. The colonies were to provide the police power to enforce the Proclamation.

To conciliate the powerful tribes of Indians in the Southern district, amounting probably to fourteen thousand fighting men, and to attach them firmly to the United States, may be regarded as highly worthy of the serious attention of Government.

The measure includes, not only peace and security to the whole southern frontier, but is calculated to form a barrier against the colonies of an European Power, which, in the mutations of policy, may one day become the enemy of the United States. The fate of the Southern States, therefore, or the neighboring colonies, may principally depend on the present measures of the Union towards the Southern Indians.

—President George Washington, in a personal appearance to request the Advice and Consent of the United States Senate, August 22, 1789.

Colonial government agents and land speculators sought to open large areas of "Indian Land" as defined by the Proclamation for settlement. Treaties were negotiated with the Iroquois (Fort Stanwix, 1768) and with the Cherokee (Hard Labor Creek, 1768 and Lochabar, 1770) for this purpose. New waves of settlers, prospectors and land speculators flowed into the Kentucky and the Ohio river valleys.

By 1773, there were 60,000 people in the Ohio Country with most of them concentrated in the area from Pittsburgh to the mouth of Ohio. There were bitter Iroquois complaints over the lack of provincial control of the traders and the traders' use of liquor during commerical transactions. Discontent was festering in the towns and councils of both the Indians and the colonists.

THE ROAD TO REVOLUTION

Pressure was placed on Great Britain to deal with the Indian "problem." More and more militia and funds were needed to quell the angry Indians who had been cheated by colonial traders along the eastern frontier. To raise revenues for colonial administration whose costs had significantly increased because of colonial and Indian wars, Britain created a series of taxation measures. Cries of "Taxation Without Representation" were heard throughout the colonies.

In addition to grievances with the Crown over taxes, the colonists complained that they were not benefiting from the democratic reforms that took place in England during the end of the 17th century. The cohesion among the colonists engendered by the French and Indian War, the common complaints against the mother country's taxation and administrative policies, and the death of the popular King George II helped spread the revolutionary fervor. In 1774, the colonies came together in a single legislative body known as the First Continental Congress to begin plans that were to result in their eventual independence from England.

INDIANS AND THE AMERICAN REVOLUTION

The first of the actual battles of the War for Independence resulted from the confrontation between the Minutemen and the British troops at Lexington on April 19, 1775. The issue was self-government. American Indian political ideas were now poised to become fatal to the monarchy.

With the outbreak of war, however, a new realization dawned on the Continental Congress about the impact of the Treaty of Paris by which the British acquired Canada in 1763. Just as the Indian nations had the option of choosing the French or the British as allies prior to 1763, the Indians now had the option of choosing the Colonies or the British government as allies. Indian rifles could be just as fatal as Indian ideas.

The Indians were viewed as an essential military element in the Revolutionary conflict. The political leaders hoped to use diplomacy to urge the Indian nations to maintain neutrality. The Colonial forces viewed the worst conceivable set of circumstances as an Indian military alliance with the British. One other alternative remained.

The Stockbridge Indians were part of the Minutemen militia. They had seen action at Lexington (April 19, 1775), Bunker Hill (June 17, 1775), the Battle of Long Island (August 19, 1775), and would continue on with Washington in other engagements through the winter of Valley Forge (1777-78). Along with the Passamaquoddy and Penobscots, the Stockbridge Indian Patriots represented the other alternative—a military alliance with the Indians.

In 1775 and 1776, the Iroquois Confederacy began to face increasing pressure from the British and Americans to take sides in the Revolutionary War. In July of 1776, Thayendanegea, the Mohawk chief who was known by the name of Joseph Brant, returned from England. Like the Stockbridge Indians, he was at the Battle of Long Island where he fought for the Crown. Thayendanegea returned to the Iroquois country and urged alliance with the British from within the Confederacy.

The Six Nations faced new appeals from all quarters to take sides in a "family quarrel" between the British and the American brothers. Under the enormous internal and external political pressures caused by divergent loyalties, the Confederacy cracked. In July, 1777, the Confederacy agreed not to agree. They would not act as the Confederacy, but were free to act as individual nations. The Confederacy had forgotten Canasatego's advice to the colonists to act in unity and never fall out with one another. Now the quarrel was between red brothers.

The Mohawks, Cayugas, Senecas, and Onondagas joined the British. The Oneidas and Tuscaroras joined the Americans. On August 6, 1777, the Oneidas and Tuscaroras rallied to the aid of American forces at Ft. Stanwix besieged by their League brothers and the British. The respective alliances were annointed with blood.

The need for an Indian role in the Revolution was seen by all American leaders. From Valley Forge on March 13, 1778, George Washington wrote to the Commissioners of Indian Affairs of his plans to use four hundred men from the Northern Tribes and the Cherokee.

And many of the Indians did fight with the Colonial forces. And so it was during that terrible winter at Valley Forge that Dr. Waldo, a surgeon, had the occasion to write:

. . . I was called to relieve a soldier thought to be dying.

He expired before I reached the hut. He was an Indian, an excellent soldier, and has fought for the very people who disinherited his forefathers.

In 1778, the Continental Congress made its very first international treaty with the Delaware Nation. Article III of that treaty engaged the Delaware in a military alliance against the British and asked this commitment from the representatives of the Delaware Nation:

And the said deputies, on behalf of their nation, engage to join the troops of the United States. . . with such a number of their best and most expert warriors as they can spare, consistent with their own safety. . . .

During the Revolution, thousands of Indians helped the colonists' cause. The Stockbridge Munsee Minutemen are but one example. These fearless warriors who taught the colonists "guerilla" tactics and aided in the Battle of Lexington lost half their troops in the Revolution. Other tribes, like the Delaware, had aided the colonists in their effort to throw off European monarchy and adopt American democracy. And of course the story of the Iroquois role is especially interesting.

MAINTAINING THE PEACE

Quite clearly in the formative years, the United States Government, operating under the Articles of Confederation, regarded peace and trade with the Indians to be critical to its survival. This was evidenced through its governing documents, official policy pronouncements and treaties.

In September, 1778, the Continental Congress concluded a treaty of alliance with the Delaware, the first treaty of the United States. The treaty embodied the three concerns that had been so much a part of the relationship between Indians and Europeans since contact: trade, land, and political relationships. Article V focused on the need for a "well-regulated trade." It was well-known that cheating traders had caused more than one Indian war on the frontier. Article VI addressed the subject of Indian land which was even more volatile than the issue of honest traders.

. . . The United States do engage to guaranty to the aforesaid nation of Delawares, and their heirs, all their territorial rights. . . .

Obviously feeling that the preceding commitments were inadequate, the United States treaty commissioners took, a final, surprising step:

And it is further agreed. . . should it. . . be found conducive fore. . . both parties to invite any other tribes who have been friends to the interest of the United States, to join the present confederation, and to form a state whereof the Delaware nation shall be the head, and have a representation in Congress. . .

This was an offer that clearly reflected the recognition by the United States of the stature of Indian governments.

When the Peace of Paris was signed with Great Britain in September, 1783, a separate peace still had to be concluded with the Indians. As a gesture of good faith, the United States issued the Proclamation of September 22, 1783. The Proclamation forbade settlement on land inhabited or claimed by the Indians outside of state jurisdiction and required any purchase or trade of such lands to be approved by Congress, declaring those transactions without such approval, null and void.

As the British had tried twenty years earlier, the committee on Indian Affairs of the confederation Congress proposed to deal with the Indians by setting firm boundary lines. Victory over the British, however, had left many of the "new" Americans land hungry and encroachment on Indian lands was widespread. The real choice facing Congress was whether to supply some minimal compensation to the Indians for their lands or finance an Indian war. Between 1778 and 1809, the United States made fifty-four treaties of "peace and friendship" with some forty tribes.

THE WAR OF 1812

The early years of the republic were tenuous. Flanked by Indian nations everywhere, the British in the Northwest, the French in New Orleans and the Spanish in Florida, they struggled to secure a faltering economy and peace. The Peace of Paris of 1783 which ended the Revolutionary War did not end the clash of interests between Britain and the United States. Spurred on by economic and boundary issues, the clash came to a head with the War of 1812.

That same year, the Shawnee chief, Tecumseh, had returned from his tour between the Great Lakes and Gulf of Mexico during which he encouraged the Indian nations to form a union to oppose United States' expansion. At once American borders felt the military power of both the Indians and the English waiting to be unleashed.

Inspired by Tecumseh's logic, the Creek chief, Red Eagle, led the Red Stick Creeks against Ft. Mims on the lower Alabama River, in August of 1813. Tennessee sent its militia after Red Eagle with General Andrew Jackson in command and Davy Crockett as a scout. Red Eagle had besieged the fort of the Talladega Creeks allied to the United States and Jackson brought his army to the aid of Talladega, but Red Eagle escaped. Federal troops under Brigadier General Claiborne, and Choctaw Nation troops under Pushmataha, moved east from Mississippi and struck Red Stick forces in Alabama.

The final clash came at Horseshoe Bend on the Tallapoosa River in Alabama in March, 1814. Jackson's troops, supported by Cherokee and Creek forces, victoriously ended the Red Stick War after a day-long battle that ended in hand to hand combat. Jackson gave a battlefield promotion to adopted Cherokee, Sam Houston.

In August, General Jackson asked the Choctaw to join his army against the British. Comissioned by the United States as a Brigadier General, Pushmataha brought a thousand Choctaws under his command to help Jackson win the Battle of New Orleans and bring the Second War of Independence to an end.

CONCLUSION

Conflict between Indian nations and the United States would continue throughout most of the 19th century as the United States expansion continued. By skillful military operations and even more skillful diplomacy, the Indian nations protected their interests as the United States grew into an overwhelming power. By 1869, the United States had concluded 370 treaties with the Indian nations which involved the purchase by the United States and sale by the Indians of nearly two billion acres of North America. These treaty negotiations left the Indian nations allied to the United States.

Despite the coercion and unscrupulous methods employed in some of these treaty negotiations, the Indian nations required the United States to pay for the land. New battles were waged in the 20th century in the court rooms of the United States, in which the United States Government acknowledged unfair dealings and made restitution to tribes through the Indian Claims Commission and the Court of Claims.

The exploits of Indian soldiers most often remembered in the 20th century are incidents from World War II. To maintain secure communications, the Marines established the Navajo Code Talkers who used their own Navajo language as a code which the enemy could never break. Navajo Tribal Chairman, Peter MacDonald served in this unit.

The most well known Indian name from World War II is that of Pima Ira H. Hayes. The sacrifices and success of the Marines in taking the Japanese held Pacific islands is memorialized by Hayes and his fellow marines in the statue atop the Iwo Jima Memorial at Arlington Cemetery.

American Indians have played the Patriors' role in United States history from the Stockbridge Minutemen at Lexington to Servicemen in Vietnam. Washington, Jefferson, Franklin, Hamilton, Madison and Jay were bold enough to try a new government inspired by concepts common to the American Indian governments that surrounded them. Indians have fought to protect the government under the United States Constitution.

In Washington, D.C. we have the Capitol, the symbol of the American seat of government and Arlington Cemetery, the symbol of sacrifice for the ideals of the American Constitution. It is appropriate that we find on the Capitol Dome the statue of the Spirit of Freedom, and at Arlington Cemetery, we find the statue of the American Indian Marine, Ira Hayes.

Osceola, the famous Seminole Chief who refused to remove to Indian Territory. He valiantly led his people in battle until the 1830s.

. . . no power ought to treat with the Indians except the United States. The Indians already know the value of confederation and were much impressed in previous years by the idea of colonial union.
—James Wilson of Pennsylvania, Debate on Management and Control of Indian Affairs, Continental Congress, July 26, 1776.

Before the revolution, the Indians were in the habit of coming often and in great numbers to the seat of government [in Virginia], where I was very much with them. I knew much the great Outcité, the warrior and orator of the Cherokee; he was always the guest of my father on his journeys to Williamsburg.
   —Thomas Jefferson to John Adams, 1812

SHAPING THE CONSTITUTION

Over the past three decades, historians and anthropologists have studied the role that Indians played in the shaping of the world's first written, shortest, and longest lasting constitution. The research is compelling; Indians did affect the formulation of that great document. Both Benjamin Franklin and Thomas Jefferson were students of politics and government; the former studied Indian forms intensively, and the latter used Indian forms in developing his rationales for self-government and personal liberty. And while the intelligentsia of the colonies was certainly familiar with the writings of Hobbs, Locke and Rousseau, there is reason to believe that the foundations of the three European theorists were Indian forms of government and social institutions.

Sir Thomas More, saint and legal philosopher, read reports of explorers like Amerigo Vespucci and envisioned a land where all men were considered equal and free, where government evolved from the will of the people rather than from the divine

In 1762, these three Cherokee chiefs carried out a diplomatic mission to London. One of them was Outicité or Man-Killer, who was often a guest of Jefferson's father. Wilma Mankiller in 1987 was elected as the first woman chief of the Cherokee in Oklahoma. Smithsonian Institution

right of kings, and where no one could be dispossessed of land he used for his sustenance. More's utopian dream kindled the intellectual fires of men like Adam Smith, Jeremy Bentham, Thomas Hobbs, John Locke, Montaigne, Montesquieu, Voltaire and Rousseau.

In another arena, reports from the New World laid the foundation for modern international law. Francisco Vitoria, professor of moral theology at the University of Salamanca, Spain, was deeply impressed by examples of Indian governments. Writing in 1532, Vitoria promoted the idea of nation to nation relationships based on reason and personal accommodations rather than religion. According to Federal Indian Law authority Felix S. Cohen, "In these and many other ways, Indian America helped to civilize Europe."

FORMS AND QUALITIES CHARACTERISTIC OF 17TH-18TH CENTURY INDIAN GOVERNMENTS

What the early reports and the writings of Franklin, Jefferson and others among the "Founders" suggest is that certain native institutional forms and socio-political qualities were: 1) totally unlike any European example, and 2) of such value as to be worked into a new democratic schema. What were these forms and qualities?

Forms

Local Self-governments
National Confederations
Elected Leaders
Popular Suffrage
Recall of Leaders
Legislative Councils Where Every Delegate Had the Right to be Heard.
Referendum
Initiative
Amendment

Qualities

Cherish Personal Freedom
Fear Personal Aggrandizement
Promote the General Welfare over Self-interest.
Mutual Accommodation
Balance and Harmony
Time to Pursue Happiness

All of these forms and qualities the founding fathers had an opportunity to see and experience in action in Indian councils of government and Indian communities where they had worked for hundreds of years.

THE ALBANY PLAN OF UNION

Amidst the growing climate of competition between France and England for Indian trade and land, the British colonies were forced to seek common solutions for dealing with the Indians and securing international trade. With the smoldering European rivalry about to erupt into the French and Indian War, the British Board of Trade instructed the royal colonial governors to meet the Six Nations at Albany in 1754 and "secure their wavering friendship." During these negotiations, representatives from the New England colonies, Pennsylvania, Maryland, and New York sought to learn everything they could about the Iroquois form of government.

During the two week period of treaty negotiations, Pennsylvania's delegate, Benjamin Franklin, presented a plan of union to the colonial representatives. The advice of Canasatego from a decade earlier was clearly on Franklin's mind as he addressed the Albany Congress.

"It would be a strange thing," he had said in 1751, "if Six Nations of ignorant savages should be capable of forming a scheme for such a union... and yet a like union should be impracticable for ten or a dozen English colonies to whom it is more necessary...."

On July 10, 1754, the colonial delegates to the Albany Congress accepted Franklin's amended Plan of Union. It was to unite all of the American colonies except Georgia and Nova Scotia. There was to be a president general appointed by the Crown and a grand council appointed by the colonial assemblies. The grand council is the name for the legislative assembly of the Iroquois Confederacy.

The president general, with the advice of the grand council, was to have a number of powers including the power to negotiate treaties, declare war, make peace with the Indians, and to regulate the Indian trade. Until the Crown created new colonies, it was to have the sole power to purchase land outside the colonies, grant land to settlers, and control the Western Territory.

The Albany Plan was rejected by both the colonists and the British for different reasons. The colonists were not prepared to give up local government to a central authority, and the British feared the political strength and independence of a centralized colonial government. The British Board of Trade proposed instead a looser union with one colonial commander-in-chief and a commissioner of Indian affairs.

FRANKLIN'S INDIAN POLICY

When the Continental Congress made Benjamin Franklin Commissioner of Indian Affairs in July, 1775, the great object of commerce and the source of controversy between the Colonies and the Indian nations was the Indians' land. The Continental Congress had moved to placate the powerful and pivotal tribes and was aware that other concessions would have to be made. Franklin's dream for a colonial parallel to the Iroquois Confederacy seemed not to have dimmed in the years since the Albany Congress. Franklin once again proposed centralized control of Indian affairs in a draft plan for confederation presented to the Continental Congress on July

Imperfect as this species of coercion may seem, crimes are very rare among them [the Indians of Virginia]; so much that were it made a question, whether no law, as among the savage Americans, or too much law, as among the civilized Europeans, submits man to the greatest evil, one who has seen both conditions of existence would pronounce it to be the last...

—Thomas Jefferson, *Notes on Virginia,* 1801.

21, 1775.

The new plan for control of Indian affairs required the consent of Congress before any colony could declare war against the Indians. It also called for a permanent alliance with the Six Iroquois Nations:

> *For them, as well as for all other tribes, boundaries should be drawn, their land protected against encroachments, and no purchases of land made except by contract drawn between the great council of the Indians and the Congress... The purchase of land from the Indians was to be "by Congress for the General Advantage and Benefit of the United colonies."*

INDIANS AND THE ROAD TO INDEPENDENCE

When the Continental Congress declared its independence from Great Britain on July 4, 1776, the Iroquois Confederacy, which called itself, "the confederacy of five fires," began to call the United States "the thirteen fires." The Iroquois' terminology more closely reflected reality than the name "United States." The thirteen colonies were united in their quest for independence, for economic growth and, for the most part, in language. In their ideas about how much power the central government should have they differed greatly.

Among the problems they had to resolve was how to deal politically and economically with the Indian nations. The principal questions that the individual colonies had to debate was how much and what kind of control should be delegated to the national legislature for Indian affairs. The answer was provided in Article IX of the Articles of Confederation, the United States' first constitution. It provided that

> *The United States in Congress assembled shall also have the sole and exclusive right and power of... regulating trade and managing all affairs with the Indians....*

Quite clearly during these formative years, the United States Government regarded the subject of trade and other relations with the Indians to be such a major concern that the subject

Tomochichi, a Creek chief, and his nephew. A friend to the English, Tomochichi helped Georgia settlers make a treaty with the lower Creek.

required special consideration in its national governing documents.

A FUNDAMENTAL RESPECT FOR THE INDIANS

The Founding Fathers, particularly Franklin, Jefferson, Washington, Patrick Henry and John Jay, had a sincere respect for the Indians—their power and political institutions. They recognized that without the help of the Indians their vision for a new democratic nation would not become a reality. Clear evidence of this respect and the stature of Indian

---

... Our legal method of compulsion is by imprisonment. The Indians cannot and will not imprison one another; and if we attempt to imprison them I apprehend it would be generally disliked by the nations, and occasion breaches. They have such high ideas of personal liberty, and such slight one of the value of personal property, that they would think the disproportion monstrous between the liberty of a man and a debt of a few shillings...

—Benjamin Franklin, 1767

government is seen in the United States' offer of statehood to the tribes, and in the development of national Indian policy and legislation.

INDIAN STATES

As we have seen in the previous chapter, the first offer of statehood was made to Delaware in the Treaty of 1778. A second offer was made to the Cherokee in Article XII of the Treaty of Hopewell, 1795.

> *That the Indians may have full confidence in the justice of the United States... they shall have the right to send a deputy of their choice... to Congress.*

This provision demonstrated how important Indian governments were to the young United States. It also indicated that the offer made to the Delaware in 1778 to form a state and take a seat in Congress was not an aberration.

Resolving the issue of peace or war with the Indian governments did not require a political alliance that would integrate the Cherokee into the United States. The purpose of the offer, rather, was to confirm "full confidence in the justice of the United States," for the United States needed the Indians as military and political allies and as trading partners.

In 1792, the Governor of Canada had proposed the creation of an Indian buffer state between British Canada and the Northwest Territory. Indian statehood was discussed again in 1830, in the Treaty with the Choctaw. In that treaty, the Choctaw requested the privilege of having a delegate in the House of Representatives. The treaty commissioners, believing it to be a matter for Congress to decide jointly, simply presented it in the treaty for consideration by Congress. Later, a congressional committee presented the proposition to Congress "with the decided opinion of the committee that it ought to receive a favorable consideration." This theme was continued after the Civil War in treaties with the Cherokee, Creek, Choctaw, Chickasaw and Seminole (popularly known as the Five Civilized Tribes) proposing the creation of an Indian State in "Indian Territory" (eastern Oklahoma).

A NEW INDIAN POLICY

Trade in goods and lands was essential for the well-being of the United States, for the fledgling government was on the verge of bankruptcy. Between the years 1774 and 1796, economic supremacy lay in the hands of the Spanish in the South and the British in the North. The United States would have to develop an effective Indian policy if it was going to break the European stranglehold and become economically viable.

Great Camp of the Pickamns near Ft. Mackenzie.

We rejoice much to learn that the great Congress have got new powers, and have become strong, we hope that whatever is done hereafter by the great council will no more be destroyed and made small by any State.
—Greetings to the United States from the Cherokee chiefs assembled at their town of Echota, May 19, 1789.

In August, 1786, Congress enacted an Ordinance for the Regulation of Indian Affairs, which set up two superintendencies in the North and the South. While they operated under the Secretary of War, their primary responsibilities were to regulate trade. The superintendent and his deputies could grant one-year licenses to American citizens permitting them to trade with the Indians. As Congress was preparing to establish the Constitutional Convention in February, 1787, Jay sent supplemental instructions to the superintendents which underlined the United States' commitment to justice and fairness in their dealing with the Indians.

In July, 1787 Congress passed the famous ordinance for the government of the Northwest Territory which formed the basis for United States-Indian dealings to the present day.

The utmost good faith shall always be observed towards the Indians; their lands and property shall never be taken from them without their consent; and in their property, rights, and liberty they never shall be invaded or disturbed unless in just and lawful wars authorized by Congress; but laws founded on justice and humanity shall from time to time be made, for preventing wrongs done to them, and for preserving peace and friendship with them.

THE CONSTITUTIONAL CONVENTION

Soon after its ratification in 1781, it became clear to many that the Articles of Confederation were not effective in allowing the national government to deal with Indians and many other matters. In May, 1787, Alexander Hamilton sent out a notice asking for delegates to attend a meeting in Philadelphia "to render the Constitution of the federal government adequate to the exigencies of the union."

Indians were not a specific major topic at the convention. According to Samuel Johnson, matters of war and peace, treaties and international relations were essentially clear among the delegates—they had to be dealt with by a strong, central government. While the delegates concentrated on matters related to getting the states to concede power to the national government, Indians were discussed when matters of international relations, making war and peace, and trade were discussed.

James Madison, "The Father of the Constitution," was determined that any new plan of union would have to overcome two major problems of the Articles of Confederation related to international relations. First, it would have to prevent the violation of the law of nation and of treaties. "The tendency of the states to these violations has been manisfested in sundry instances. The files of Congress contain complaints already from almost every nation with which treaties have been formed."

Second, it would have to prevent encroachments on the Federal Authority. "By the Federal Articles, transactions with the Indians appertain to Congress; yet in several instances the states have entered into treaties and wars with them...without the consent of Congress."

The draft of the constitution presented on August 6, 1787 did not address Indian affairs. The details of too many other issues had obviously preoccupied the convention. Finally, on August 18, 1787, Madison pressed for unrestricted jurisdiction over Indian affairs on the part of Congress. His motion was reworked in committee and emerged in Article I, Section 8, "the Commerce Clause" which simply states:

The Congress shall have Power To...regulate Commerce with foreign Nations, and among the several States, and with the Indian Tribes.

A Creek leader who visited President Washington in New York in 1790 to discuss land cessions. The artist, John Trumbull, described him as having "a dignity of manner...worthy of a Roman senator."

THE FEDERALIST PAPERS

After Benjamin Franklin skillfully brought the convention to an end with the signing of the Constitution by the Delegates on September, 1787, the most difficult job remained—educating the public so that they might ratify the document. Indians, known for their oratory, would have resorted to speech making. Alexander Hamilton, James Madison, and John Jay sought to inform and influence through writing. In a series of eighty-five essays known as *The Federalist Papers* published in 1788, they brilliantly defended the revolutionary charter, the Constitution of the United States. Several of these mentioned Indians.

In the third Federalist Paper, written in fall, 1787, John Jay discussed the failing of the Articles of Confederation and the wars that had resulted from the states acting in an area reserved for the national government.

Not a single Indian war has yet been produced by aggresions of the present federal government, feeble as it is; but there are several instances of Indian hostilities having been provoked by the improper conduct of individual States, who, either unable or unwilling to restrain or punish offenses, have given occasion to the slaughter of many innocent inhabitants.

In numbers 24 and 25 of the Federalist Papers, Hamilton used the example of Indian military strength and political alliances to defend the provision of a "common defense" by the national government.

Madison addressed the need for the Commerce Clause in Federalist Paper No. 42. The Articles of Confederation had sought to regulate Indian trade by restraining the Indians but not the citizens of the various states. The United States Constitution, in contrast, gave jurisdiction with respect to Indian trade solely to the central government, not to the states.

TRADE AS BASIS FOR FEDERAL INDIAN POLICY

Since the early 1700s the policy of the European governments in attempting to influence Indians had centered on trade, as summarized by this British view:

To preserve the balance between us and the French is the great ruling principal of modern Indian politics. The Indian frequently repeated that trade was the foundation of the alliance or connexion with us and that it is the chief cement which binds us together and this should undoubtedly be the first principal of our whole system of Indian politics.

These principles remained just as true for the United States in 1789. On March 4, 1789, the Constitution of the United States went into effect. The United States Government, operating under its new Constitution, fully intended to use commerce and the whole economic relationship with the tribes as a political tool. The commercial theme would appear time and time again in statutes and treaties defining the relationship with the Indian nations. And although these pronouncements would talk of the necessity of adopting such policies for the well-being of the Indians, the policies also were adopted with the well-being of the United States in mind. If the United States were to prosper, American merchants needed an Indian market for their goods and needed to assume the middleman role between the Indians and Europe to extract profits from the fur trade. Ultimately it would succeed in obtaining both the Spanish and the British trade and most of the Indians' land.

Historian Samuel Eliot Morrison noted in his *History of the American People* that, "Washington and Congress were as deeply concerned over Indian as European relations." Soon after taking office, President Washington wrote to the Senate concerning "disputes...between some of the United States and several powerful tribes of Indians." On that date Congress reenacted the Northwest Ordinance pledging "of utmost good faith" in their dealings with the Indians. On that date also Congress established the War Department and assigned to the Secretary all matters relative to Indian affairs "entrusted to him by the President of the United States, agreeably to the Constitution...."

On August 20, 1789, heeding the firm advice of Secretary of War, Henry Knox, to purchase the Indian land rather than to occupy it according to the theory of conquest, Congress appropriated $20,000 for negotiating and treating.

Congress also took steps to regulate commerce with the Indians by passing the first of the series of Trade and Intercourse acts. In the Act of July 22, 1790, the President was given the

---

We are of the same opinion with the people of the United States; you consider yourselves as independent people; we, as the original inhabitants of this country, and sovereigns of the soil, look upon ourselves as equally independent, and free as any other nation or nations.

—Joseph Brant, Mohawk Chief, to the United States Treaty Commissioners, April 21, 1794.

necessary authority to issue regulations governing all trade or intercourse with the tribes. The Act also specified the exclusive right of the United States Government to purchase Indian lands, and no sale of land by Indians was to be valid "unless the same shall be duly executed at some public treaty, held under the authority of the United States."

WASHINGTON'S INDIAN POLICY

The themes of political and economic alliance with the Indians remained prominent in President Washington's messages to Congress. In his annual message in October, 1791, he stated proposals "to advance the happiness of the Indians and to attach them firmly to the United States." His proposal included:

1. A carefully defined and regulated method of purchasing lands from the Indians and

2. Promotion of commerce with the Indians, "under regulations tending to secure an equitable deportment toward them."

Since the troubles with Indian traders and trespass on Indian land continued in the western borders, Congress saw the need to continue the regulation of Indian trade and passed the second Indian Trade and Intercourse Act on March 1, 1793. In his annual message in December of that year, Washington continued his theme of political and economic alliance with the Indians. Speaking of his anxiety over the tenuous peace with the Creeks and the Cherokees "and the critical footing on which we stand in regard to these tribes," he said, "It is with Congress to pronounce what shall be done." His recommendations for action included creating "ties of interest" and "rigorous execution of justice upon the violators" of federal laws and treaties.

In April, 1796, Congress authorized the President "to establish trading houses at such posts and places...convenient for the purpose of carrying on a liberal trade with the several Indian nations." Washington's plans for cementing political alliances with the Indians was underway. The government trading houses would protect the Indians and the United States from the consequences of the abuses of the private traders.

Since intrusions on the Cherokee and Creek nations caused the southwestern border to simmer, the first trading house was established among the southern Indians. In 1806, the post of Superintendent of Indian Trade was created by statute. Government trading houses were a non-profit enterprise developed as part of a diplomatic plan of the United States to engage a favorable alliance with the Indian nations. But what the United States could do for cost, others could do for profit, and opposition to the trading houses began to build. By abolishing the trading houses in 1822, federal Indian policy was shaped for the benefit of private economic needs, rather than for the needs of the general populace.

CONCLUSION

As the new government got under way, it was clear that concepts about Indian government and Indian policy shaped the development of the Constitution. Indians were the southern and western borders of the United States. Relationships with them could not be ignored and were not. The presence of the Indians shaped the world of the new United States, as their presence had shaped the world of the colonists. The imprint of Indian America was on the Constitution.

Austenaco, one of the principal chiefs of the Cherokee accompanied Outicité to London in 1762 on a diplomatic mission which resulted in an English-Cherokee treaty in 1763.

When European colonial powers began to explore and colonize this land, they entered into treaties with sovereign Indian nations. Our new nation continued to make treaties and to deal with Indian tribes on a government-to-government basis. Throughout our history, despite periods of conflict and shifting national policies in Indian affairs, the government-to-government relationship between the United States and Indian tribes has endured. The Constitution, treaties, laws, and court decisions have consistently recognized a unique political relationship between Indian tribes and the United States which this Administration pledges to uphold.

—President Ronald Reagan,
Indian Policy Statement, January 24, 1983.

INDIANS UNDER THE CONSTITUTION

In those times after the Constitution had just been written and while the men who had written that document held positions in the American government, Indian governments were perceived as institutions on a par with the United States Government. The Indian nations were the object of military, economic and political alliances. In the face of the bitter hostility of the southern states, engendered because of economic pressures and racial prejudice, the political fortunes of the southern tribes faded. Across the Mississippi they would try to resurrect those faded fortunes.

And for a time fortune did smile on the eastern tribes in their Oklahoma homes, and on the mighty military tribes of the Great Plains. Westward expansion however, placed their way of life and land in jeopardy by the Centennial of the Constitution. As the 20th century started, the power of the Constitution would bring the tribes back from the brink of disaster and shape Indian policy as the Founding Fathers envisioned.

Delegation from several Indian tribes at the White House, on December 31, 1857.

WESTWARD EXPANSION

As the young United States Government attempted to consolidate its power in North America and stabilize and strengthen its national government, its Indian policy shifted focus from trade in goods to trade in land. President Washington had moved to deal with Indian trade and treaties only a few days after becoming president. When internal United States political pressures called for rapid territorial expansion, President Jefferson shifted federal Indian policy from economic alliance to *assimilation* or *removal*. The tribes were forced to leave their homes in the East to the distant lands across the Mississippi.

THE REMOVAL POLICY

It is not an accident that today a majority of Indian tribes are located west of the Mississippi River. For much of the first half of the 19th century, both the President and the Congress yielded to public pressure for more of the Indians' land and valuable resources.

The seeds for removal began early, as the young nation sought to meet the needs and demands of its growing population. Boundary lines began to change. Under the Treaty of Greenville, August 3, 1795, the Wyandot, Delaware, Shawnee, Ottawa, Chippewa, Potawatomi, Miami, Wea, Kickapoo, Piankashaw, and Kaskaskia of the Northwest gave up most of Ohio and Indiana and the settlements of Vicennes, Detroit and Chicago.

In 1803, the Louisiana Purchase was made from France which enabled President Jefferson to promote the removal policy. The Louisiana Purchase (Article IV) required the United States to honor treaties with the Indian nations or renegotiate them if the Indians agreed to do so. Fort Smith (Arkansas) was established in 1817 and Ft. Gibson (Oklahoma) was developed in 1826 to aid in dealing with the Indians.

Between 1817 and 1823, the first wave of Cherokee migration moved into Arkansas and Oklahoma from Georgia and Tennessee. When Sam Houston resigned as governor of Tennessee, he joined his Cherokee family there and started a trading post. He found himself in Washington challenging his mentor, President Jackson, over Indian issues. By the time he left Oklahoma for Texas in 1833, rumors were rampant that Jackson,

Houston and the Cherokee were plotting to establish an Indian Empire in Texas with Houston as emperor.

In 1819, the United States acquired Florida and the Oregon Country from Spain and Secretary of War Calhoun issued an order creating the Bureau of Indian Affairs. Indian nations were losing political leverage with the loss of potential foreign allies. The prosperous farms of the Five Civilized Tribes were coveted by their white neighbors. Gold was discovered on the Cherokee land in Georgia and greed promoted the passage of the 1830 Indian Removal Act. Congressman Davy Crockett of Tennessee voted against President Jackson's Indian Removal Act because he thought it was immoral. The stage was set for a conflict between Georgia and the Cherokee.

In the 1820s the Cherokee transformed their government. They moved from the town governments to a centralized government, and in 1827 adopted a written constitution modeled after the United States Constitution. The document that the Indians had inspired was now a source of inspiration.

The very idea of civilized and responsible Indians in the Cherokee Republic was repugnant to the southern governors. It would undermine all propaganda of the Indians as "savages" and undermine the removal policy. Georgia challenged the Cherokee and the result was two court cases that shaped federal-Indian relation up to the present day.

GEORGIA AND THE CHEROKEE BEFORE THE SUPREME COURT

Georgia asserted jurisdiction over the Cherokee people and lands within the State. The Cherokee saw Georgia's action as an attack on the United States Constitution and the Cherokee treaties as the Supreme Law of the land. When the dispute went before the Supreme Court in 1831 in *Cherokee Nation v. Georgia,* United State Chief Justice John Marshall sidestepped the issue. He declared that the Supreme Court did not have original jurisdiction because the Cherokee were not an independent foreign nation but a "domestic, dependent nation." In this first attempt to define the relationship between Indian governments and the United States the Court also said, "The relation to the United States resembles that of a ward to his guardian," providing a basis for the United States "trust relationship" with Indian tribes.

When the Reverend Samuel Worcester, translating the Bible into Cherokee on the Cherokee Reservation, failed to take an oath of allegiance to the State of Georgia, he was convicted of violating Georgia law and sentenced to four years of hard labor. The case of *Worcester v. Georgia,* was decided by the Supreme Court in 1832.

This time the Court did not hesitate to assert federal jurisdiction over the State. Chief Justice Marshall noted that the legal and political status of the Cherokee and all other Indian tribes was as *"distinct, independent political communities."* He also said that within the boundaries of the Cherokee Nation *"the laws of Georgia can have no force"* and that such laws were "repugnant to the constitution, treaties, and laws of the United States...."

Political pressure in the conflict of state sovereignty versus federal supremacy threatened to shatter the federal Union and overwhelmed the Cherokee legal victory. South Carolina had passed legislation to "nullify" a federal tariff. When the Cherokee assessed the situation, it appeared that if they pushed Jackson to enforce the *Worcester* decision, other southern states would side with South Carolina and a civil war would follow. The Cherokee decided to sacrifice their homeland rather than the United States. The *Worcester* case was dropped. For the Five Civilized Tribes the Southeast United States would no longer be home. The Choctaw were forced west in 1831, the Creek in 1836, the Chickasaw in 1837, and the Cherokee in 1838-39 in the bitter "Trail of Tears." Finally the Seminole were forced west in 1842.

PEACE ON THE PLAINS

A decade after the Five Civilized Tribes had been pushed west the United States was at peace with Mexico with an established border. Sam Houston had built his Texas empire but without his beloved Cherokee. The U.S. had also settled its border dispute with Britain in the Oregon Country. There was even peace with the Indians for in 1849 the Bureau of Indian Affairs had been moved from the military control of the War Department to civilian control in the newly created Interior Department.

If the peaceful relations were to be maintained with the Indians of the Plains in the 1850s, the United States would have to shore up an unstable peace whose balance was being affected by the settlers trespassing on Indian land on their way to Oregon and California. The United States diplomatic tool was the treaty-making authority of the Constitution.

The reputation of the Plains Indians as fighters indicated that a peace treaty was in order. The Northern Plains tribes were considered formidable by sheer numbers alone. The United States knew it had to have their cooperation. The tribes of the Southern Plains had held the Mexicans, Texans, and Americans at bay for years. One of their cavalry opponents called them the "finest light cavalry in the world." The cooperation of the Indian Nations was requested by the United States in the treaties of 1850s in which the United States compensated the Plains tribes for the trouble of putting up with the while immigrants passing through Indian country.

The Civil War momentarily distracted the United States Government from Indian affairs. Southern diplomacy on Indian affairs pulled Cherokee Stand Watie into the Confederate Army as a Brigadier General. In the stillness at Appomattox General Grant's aide, Brigadier General Eli Parker, a Tonawanda Seneca, drafted the articles of surrender that General Lee would sign. President Grant would appoint General Parker as Commissioner of Indian Affairs in 1869. The next time a president would put an

Indian in control of Indian affairs would be in 1966 when President Johnson appointed Oneida Robert Bennett as Commissioner of Indian Affairs. When the Civil War was settled, the federal government would turn its attention back to the Indians and their lands.

The post-Civil War American frontier of 1865 consisted of one million unsettled square miles stretching from St. Louis to the Pacific Ocean. The 100,000 Indians in the area would clash with the United States in the final struggle for the American West. In the Great Plains the army had to face Sioux, Blackfeet, Crow, Mandan, Arikara, Cheyenne, Arapaho, Kiowa and Comanche. In the Rocky Mountains, Nez Perce, Ute, Shoshone, and Bannock posed an obstacle to white expansion. Beyond the Rocky Mountains the Paiute and Modoc were the foe. In the Southwest the Navajo and Apache opposed the invasion of their homeland.

The military power of the tribes was so frustrating to some United States officials that extermination was offered as the final solution of the "Indian problem." Use of the Constitutional war powers may have been legal but it was not practical. Maintenance of troops alone was costing $2 million a year. The 1870 estimate was that Indian wars had cost the government more than $1 million for every dead Indian. President Washington and Secretary of War Knox had warned against the costs of Indian wars a century before.

To achieve Peace on the Plains the Great Peace Commission was sent out for one last round of treaty making in 1867 and 1868. The tribes did not lose the wars as much as they lost the peace which followed. Although Congress by statute declared that it would no longer make "treaties" with the Indians in 1871 because of an internal dispute between the House and Senate over financial obligations in Indian treaties, the United States continued to strike land deals with the Indian governments but referred to them as "agreements." This was done so that both the House and Senate were involved in ratification rather than just the Senate. The format changed but the Constitutional consequences remained the law of the land. The last of this series of agreements was negotiated in 1911.

THE ALLOTMENT POLICY

The various economic interests such as the railroads, land speculators, ranchers, farmers, large mineral companies, and mustered out Civil War veterans combined to force the United States Government to formulate a policy that would open up the private lands of Indians and the public lands of the United States for further exploitation. By the end of the 19th century the articulated Indian policy developed fully into that of "allotment in severalty." This meant dividing up the reservations into homestead allotments for the Indians, declaring unallotted lands "surplus" to Indian needs and declaring these surplus lands available to white homesteaders.

The Centennial of the Constitution was no cause for

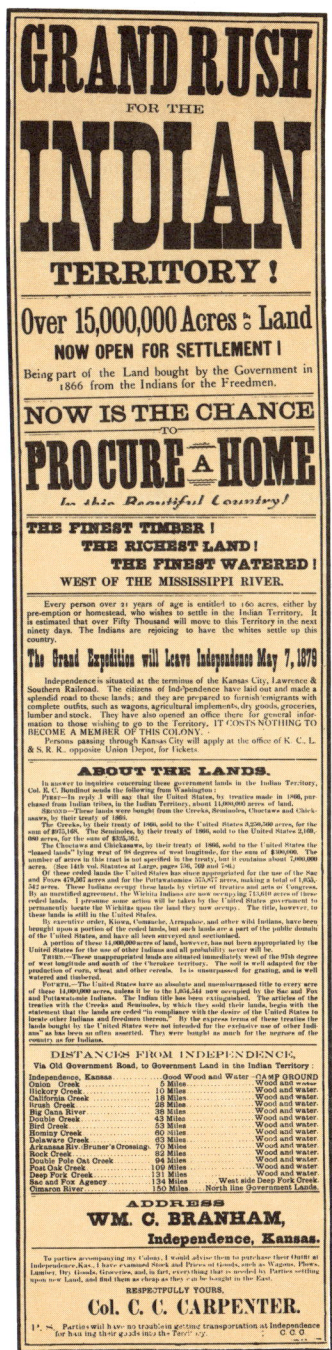

Land Rush advertisement offering 15 million acres in Indian Territory. Includes lands formerly held by the Creek, Choctaw, Chickasaw, Seminole, Kiowa, Comanche, Arapaho, "and other wild Indians," and the Potowatomie.

celebration for Indians. Senator Dawes pushed through Congress the General Allotment Act of 1887 which was intended to open more Indian lands for white settlement and assimilate all Indians into American society. The Indian land base shrank from 140 million acres in 1887 to 50 million acres in 1934. The Allotment Policy affected the strength and cohesiveness of Indian governments because the Act transferred control of Indian land and resources to Bureau of Indian Affairs administrators. Bureaucrats controlled Indian money, wills, choice of attorneys, and leasing of land and resources. The policies tht had broken up the Indian land base shattered the Indian economy, the governmental structures, and attacked tribal cultures. By the Centennial of the Constitution, the United States role as trustee of Indian economic and political interests had shifted in character and the protector had become a virtual dictator.

THE BUREAUCRATIC DICTATORSHIP

After the Great Peace Commission Indians continued to capture the attention of the public. During the centennial celebration of the Declaration of Independence on June 25, 1876, Colonel George Armstrong Custer exhibited the singularly bad judgment of attacking with his six hundred men a vastly numerically superior and better armed camp of Sioux and their Cheyenne allies enjoying their summer vacation on the Little Big Horn River. The United States Government set out to kill all the Sioux or force them onto a reservation. Sitting Bull escaped to Canada but returned in 1881 to join Buffalo Bill Cody's Wild West Show and tour the United States and Europe.

It was during this continued national focus on the Sioux in 1883 that Crow Dog killed Spotted Tail, the nationally famous chief of the Brule Sioux, within the Sioux reservation. Crow Dog was punished according to Sioux law, but Dakota Territory also tried him for murder. Crow Dog challenged his death sentence and the United States Supreme Court held that only an Indian government can punish an Indian for committing a crime against another Indian. The Court pointed out that under the 1834 Trade and Intercourse Act Indian nations retained authority over their domestic or internal affairs, including the punishment of members of of the tribe who violated tribal law. This sovereign power of Indian ntions had not been surrendered by later treaties according to the Court.

The non-Indian public was outraged and Congress in 1885 passed the Major Crimes Act which authorized federal jurisdiction over seven crimes in Indian Country including murder committed by one Indian against another. In the 1886 case of *United States v. Kagama,* the United States Supreme Court upheld the authority of Congress to pass the legislation. In this case the Supreme Court lost sight of the Constitution as a source for United States' authority in Indian affairs and offered in its place a rationale of "the course of dealing with the Federal Government" with the Indians.

These two cases promoted the idea that Congress had absolute, despotic power over Indians. Supreme Court decisions of the next century had to remind Congress and the Bureau of Indian Affairs that the Constitution imposed limitations on federal power over Indian nations.

In those decades before and after the year 1900 one would have been hardpressed to identify Constitutional limitations on Federal power over Indians. In the Southern Plains in 1890, the Indian Agent sent cavalry troops to stop the Sun Dance religious celebration of the Kiowas. The Annual Report of the Commissioner of Indian Affairs for the Year 1901 described an incident from 1900 involving the Northern Cheyenne medicine man, Porcupine, who was reported reviving the "Messiah craze" of the Ghost Dance religion of the 1890s. Fearful of Porcupine's influence, Indian agent James Clifford reported that Porcupine's religious activities and presence were "detrimental to the peace and welfare of the Indians." Clifford recommended that Porcupine be "taken under guard and turned over to the commanding officer of Fort Keogh for confinement at hard labor... until such time as he shall be thoroughly disciplined and taught to respect and obey officers of the Government...."

The Secretary of War finally agreed to the Department of the Interior's request and Porcupine was arrested and taken away to Ft. Keogh. One can be certain that the issues of due process, religious freedom, and freedom of speech never crossed the mind of Indian Agent Clifford.

Using the absolute power from the *Kagama* decision, Congress dropped the 1867 idea of developing an Indian state in Oklahoma and passed the Curtis Act in 1898 with the goal of terminating the affairs of the Five civilized Tribes, dismantling their tribal governments, and opening their lands and declaring the remaining land surplus to Indian needs and available to homesteaders, cattlemen, businesses, railroads, and mineral companies interested in the oil, coal, and other resources.

The Curtis Act established the Dawes Commission or the Commission to the Five Civilized Tribes which was to conduct negotiations with these tribes. The self-governing Five Civilized Tribes were negotiating agreements with the Dawes Commission in 1900 about the final disposition of their affairs. The target date

The treaties and the laws of the United States contemplate the Indian territory as completely separated from that of the states; and provide that all intercourse with them shall be carried on exclusively by the government of the union.
—Chief Justice John Marshall, *Cherokee Nation v. Georgia, 1831.*

for the end of the governments of the Five Civilized Tribes was March of 1906, but the business affairs of the tribe were not completed by the deadline. In the debate to amend the deadline, Congress discovered that it had no idea what it had done to the Five Civilized Tribes. Faced with this situation, Congress rejected termination and passed legislation that continued the tribal existence and the governments of the Five Civilized Tribes.

The Bureau of Indian Affairs ignored Congress, pretended the governments of the Five Civilized Tribes did not exist, and ran the affairs of the tribes as an administrative dictatorship. Federal courts reviewing the unlawful conduct of Bureau of Indian Affairs officials in 1976, said that the attitude of federal officials "can only be characterized as bureaucratic imperialism."

THE CONSTITUTION SUPPORTS INDIAN GOVERNMENT IN THE 20TH CENTURY

Despite the political, economic and social devastation to Indian tribes caused by federal policies and legislation during the 19th and early 20th centuries, the Constitution was working for Indians in certain respects. Of course, there had been the confirmation of Indian governmental sovereignty by the Supreme Court in *Worcester v. Georgia*, in 1832. In 1905, the Court ruled that the taxing power of the Creek was an inherent sovereign power. The Court ruled in 1912 that the Indian homestead allotments which the Federal Government had initiated with a guarantee of no taxes was a vested property right protected by the Fifth Amendment to the Constitution. While Congress, in 1924, passed the Indian Citizenship Act to make all Indians citizens of the United States yet preserve their rights as tribal citizens, it took a 1948 lawsuit to force New Mexico to allow Indians to vote.

The Roosevelt New Deal was extended to Indians through the work of Commissioner of Indian Affairs John Collier and the Associate Solicitor for Indian Affairs, Felix Cohen. The 1934 Indian Reorganization Act revitalized the Indian nations by recognizing the authority of Indian governments, placing restraints on federal powers applied to Indians, stopping the loss of Indian lands, and establishing economic development programs for tribes. It recognized Indian sovereign powers and assisted tribes with establishing written constitutions and laws. Collier understood that non-Indians did not believe Indian governments were "real" without these written documents.

Implementation of the Indian Reorganization Act was delayed by administrative politics, congressional misgivings, lack of support by suspicious Indian leaders, and attacks by white ranchers, farmers, and businessmen. It was forgotten entirely during World War II. The resurgence of tribal governments that Collier and Cohen envisioned did not transpire until after the Termination Policy of the 1950s lost its luster, and proved a social and economic disaster for the tribes.

The last three decades have seen strong positive policies towards Indians. President Johnson's War on Poverty brought vital economic resources into Indian country. In 1970, President Nixons's Message on Indian affairs represented one of the most positive Indian statements of the century.

And in keeping with his support of Indian self-determination, President Reagan appointed in 1981 the first Indian physician to head the Public Health Service's Indian Health Service. He is Dr. Everett Rhoades, a member of the Kiowa Tribe. President Reagan's Indian policy statement of 1983 was reminiscent of the days when George Washington emphasized the need for political and economic alliance between the United States and Indian Nations.

The United States began to resurrect the treaty negotiations for Indian land when it discovered the land was not purchased properly in accordance with the 1834 Trade and Intercourse Act. In 1971, Congress passed the Alaska Native Claims Settlement Act. In 1978, Congress approved the Rhode Island Indian Claims Settlement Act with the Narragansett Tribe. And in 1980, the Passamaquoddy, Penobscot and Maliseet negotiated a settlement with Maine in the Maine Indian Claims Settlement. Poised to begin celebrating the Constitution's bicentennial, Congress, in July 1987, extended the unique federal—Indian trust relationship to the Alabama-Coushatta and Tigua tribes located in Texas.

Indian governments have seen positive responses from the United States Supreme Court in these same decades. In 1978, the Court ruled in *Santa Clara Pueblo v. Martinez* that due process and equal protection principles of the 1968 Indian Civil Rights Act must be decided in a manner consistent with traditional Indian values and customs. That same year in *United States v. Wheeler*, the Court ruled that Indian tribes remain separate political communities with the inherent power to enact laws and prosecute tribal members.

All the old movies and television shows said the Indian treaties were broken. Many people also assumed that since these treaties were so old they had no power. In 1979, as it considered the Washington State fishing cases, the Supreme Court pointed out that United States treaties with Indians are contracts "between

---

The constitution, declaring treaties already made, as well as those to be made, to be the supreme law of the land, has adopted and sanctioned the previous treaties with the Indian nations, and consequently admits their rank among those powers who are capable of making treaties.

—Chief Justice John Marshall, *Cherokee Nation v. Georgia*, 1831.

two sovereign nations." The Court ruled the treaties were still valid. If age suspends a law then the United States Constitution would have no authority. People have forgotten that breaking a law does not invalidate the law, it only means there may be consequences if one is caught. The same is true of treaties.

In 1987, in *California v. Cabazon Band of Mission Indians* the United States Supreme Court ruled that the State of California did not have jurisdiction in Indian Country. This kind of decision reaches back to the days of *Worcester v. Georgia* in 1832. Indian governments have not lost their aspirations to govern themselves and State governments continue to attack Indian governmental authority.

The source of authority for the role of the Federal Government in Indian affairs is the Commerce Clause and the Treaty Clause of the United States Constitution. This was true in the time of the Founding Fathers and it remains true today. The Supreme Court has had to remind Americans periodically that there are Constitutional limitations on the Federal Government's power in Indian affairs, "The power of Congress over Indian affairs may be of a plenary nature; but it is not absolute."

Seventeen-tribe council held in 1843 at the new Cherokee Capitol in Tahlequah, Indian Territory. Called by Cherokee Chief John Ross to promote friendship among their new neighbors, the Council was attended by 10,000 delegates.

From the American Indian the government of the Founding Fathers received many gifts. The Indians shared the resources of the United States, they revealed that the true wealth of America was its liberty and spirit of freedom, and they demonstrated new governmental principles in operation that were far different from any European monarchy. The Indians offered essential political, economic, and military alliances at critical times, such as during the War for Independence. The United States has pledged of "utmost good faith" in its dealing with Indian governments. The Founding Fathers pledged justice and the honor of the United States.

The American Indian, by 1787, had well established his importance in the early history of the United States and the formation of its Constitution. By 1987, the United States Constitution had established its importance to American Indians by providing protection of Indian lands, treaty rights, and the tribal right of self government. While the government to government relationship has not always been smooth, Indian rights as "important national principles" live today under the United States Constitution as the Founding Fathers envisioned.

Column of cavalry, artillery, and wagons commanded by Col. George A. Custer, crossing the plains of Dakota Territory.

When we forget great contributors to our American history—when we neglect the heroic past of the American Indian—we thereby weaken our own heritage. We need to remember the contributions our forefathers found here and from which they borrowed liberally.

—President John F. Kennedy, 1961.

BIBLIOGRAPHY

Adair, James. *History of the American Indians*. Samual C. Williams, editor. 1775 reprint. New York: Johnson, 1969.

Brandon, William. *The Last Americans*. New York: McGraw Hill, 1974.

Cohen, Felix. *The Legal Conscience*. New Haven, Connecticut: Yale University Press, 1960.

Colden, Cadwallader. *The History of the Five Nations Depending on the Province of New York in America*. 1727 and 1747 reprint. Ithaca, New York: Cornell University Press, 1958.

DeRosier, Arthur, Jr. *The Removal of the Choctaw Indians*. Knoxville, Tennessee: University of Tennessee Press, 1970.

Franklin, Benjamin. "Remarks Concerning the Savages." Volume x. In *The Writings of Benjamin Franklin*. Albert Henry Smith, editor. New York: Macmillan Company, 1905.

Hamilton, Alexander, James Madison, and John Jay. *The Federalist Papers*. New York: The New American Library, Inc., 1961.

Jefferson, Thomas. *Notes on the State of Virginia*. New York: Furman and Loudon, 1801.

Jefferson, Thomas. *The Jefferson Cyclopedia*. New York, 1901.

Jennings, Francis. *The Invasion of America*. New York: W.W. Norton and Company, Inc., 1976.

Johansen, Bruce. *Forgotten Founders*. Ipswitch, Massachusetts: Gambit Inc., 1982.

Josephy, Alvin M., Jr. (ed.). *The American Heritage Book of Indians*. New York: The American Heritage Publishing Co., 1961.

McLoughlin, William G. *Cherokee Renascence in the New Republic*. Princeton, New Jersey: Princeton University Press.

Montaigne, Michel de. "Of the Cannibals." In *The Complete Essays of Montaigne*. Donald H. Frame, translator. Stanford, California: Stanford University Press, 1948.

Morgan, Lewis Henry. *League of the Iroquois*. New York: Corinth Books, 1962.

Morison, Samuel Eliot. *The Oxford History of the American People*. Volumes I, II, III. New York: New American Library, 1972.

Padover, Saul K. *The Complete Jefferson*. New York: Duell, Sloan and Pearce, Inc., 1943.

Padover, Saul K. *To Secure These Blessings*. New York: Washington Square Press and Ridge Press, 1962.

Parker, Arthur C. *The Constitution of the Five Nations*. New York State Museum Bulletin. Albany, New York: New York State Museum, 1916.

Richardson, James D., comp. *A Compilation of the Messages and Papers of the Presidents*. Volume I. Washington, D.C.: n.Publ., 1896-1899.

Schlesinger, Arthur. *Almanac of American History*. New York: Bramhall House, 1983.

Swanton, John R. *Source Material for the Social and Ceremonial Life of the Choctaw Indians*. Bureau of American Ethnology Bulletin 103. Washington, D.C., 1931.

Swanton, John R. *The Indians of the Southeastern United States*. Bureau of American Ethnology Bulletin 137. New York: Greenwood Press, 1946.

The Great Law of Peace of the Longhouse People. Rooseveltown, New York: Akwesasne Notes and Mohawk Nation, 1977.

Van Doren, Carl. *Benjamin Franklin*. New York: Bramhall House, 1938.

About the Author's

Kirke Kickingbird. Executive Director and co-founder of the Institute for the Development of Indian law and Kiowa tribal member, Mr. Kickingbird is considered an authority on Federal Indian Law and tribal government. A member of the Oklahoma and District of Columbia Bars and the Federal Tax Court, he has conducted hundreds of seminars, over 20 research projects, and written extensively in the field of Federal Indian Law. His writings include a book, *One Hundred Million Acres* (Macmillan Company, 1973), and "In Our Image...After Our Likeness: The Drive for the Assimilation of Indian Court Systems," *(American Criminal Law Review,* 1976). **Lynn Shelby Kickingbird** has co-authored several books and articles with her husband. She is managing editor of the Institute's publications department.

About the Institute for the Development of Indian Law
Founded in 1971 by three Indian attorneys, the Institute is a non-profit, tax-exempt action research organization devoted to strengthening the rights of Indian people through legal and historical research, training, and publication. This Institute's publications division currently offers 77 titles and 10 videos.

KF 8205 .Z9 K43

Kickingbird

Indians and the U.S. Constitution

Publications of the Institute for the Development of Indian Law

THE AMERICAN INDIAN JOURNAL — A quarterly publication containing well-researched, yet easily understood, articles relating to Indian life, history, government and law. **The Washington Report** section provides current information about pending legislation, policy decisions, regulatory activities, court decisions and "Indian News around the country."
Price: $50 annual subscription, $69 out of country

BOOKS ON FEDERAL INDIAN LAW

- *Indian Sovereignty* $10
- *Indian Jurisdiction* $12
- *Introduction to Oil and Gas* $12
- *Indian Treaties* $10
- *Indian Water Rights* $12
- *Federal Indian Trust Relationship* $15

PROCEEDINGS OF THE GREAT PEACE COMMISSION $10

Featuring treaty negotiations of the Sioux, Comanche, Kiowa, Apache, Navajo, Shoshone, Bannock, Cheyenne and Osage durig the critical year, 1868.

BICENTENNIAL EDUCATION KIT

Intended for a variety of audiences from high-school to adult:
- *Two-color brochure* .25 ea., discounts available
- *40-page booklet* 7.95 (discounts for 10 or more)
- *15-minute video* 125.00 (special price with this ad)

(Discounts Available to schools and libraries)

Call or Write:
Institute for the Development of Indian Law
1104 Glyndon Street, S.E.
Vienna, VA 22180
(703) 938-7822

Ask about our:
Treaty Books • Treaty Manuscript Collection
Films & filmstrips • High School curriculum

5% discount on all orders with cash payment. All orders of $100 or more require 50% deposit. Add 5% to all orders for postage and handling.